3030

NEW PHOTOGRAPHY

IN CHINA

3030

NEW PHOTOGRAPHY

IN CHINA

Ed. John Millichap

3030 Press

Introduction

Since the mid-1990s, Chinese society has undergone an astonishing transformation, unprecedented in the modern world and marked by the embrace of consumerism, both as an ideology and as the main value system of daily life. Today, an entire generation in China can look back on lives lived entirely against the backdrop of economic change; the first in modern China whose life experiences, values and behaviour are based on consumer ideology – what might be described as China's first generation of individualistic "new citizens".

It is a generation whose sensibilities and character are utterly distinct and for whom the power of the image is paramount. Images of consumerism, endlessly transformed are delivered through all forms of the mass media, both foreign information sources as well as the vast majority of Chinese media whose version of foreign-style consumption is intended to epitomise some kind of globalised new life ideal. Significantly, it is China's young generation that is most deeply affected by this, and in its pursuit of this new ideal has been led to a version of individualism that differs totally from anything in any previous generation in modern China. As a result, any consideration of new photography, so-called "personal photography", must also begin with China's social transformation.

The popularization of photography in daily life began in the 1980s as living standards and personal wealth gradually increased. Already, China was saturated by consumer-style images, both home grown and imported, so the adoption of photography as the main means of self-expression, particularly by the young, is perhaps unsurprising. Mass communication and the Internet only served to hasten this process by offering even more possibilities for self-expression. As the quality of digital technology increased and costs continued to fall, China's urban youth found itself in possession of the kind of technology that would have been unthinkable only a few years previously. As a result, photography became a new kind of "language" for the expression of the individual.

From a certain perspective, the emergence of personal photography in China is closely related to the sudden rise of new generation photography in Guangdong and the province's dynamic mass media. An entire group of young photographers emerged during the first Yipin Photography Festival in 2001 and the Pingyao International Photography Festival a year later. Many of them have links to the region's mass media, either as contributors or as staff reporters and photographers.

During the Yipin festival a series of attention-grabbing satellite shows, organized by established photographer-curators including Yan Changjiang, Wang Ningde, Ya Niu and Zeng Yicheng, among others, became a target for criticism from the national press. An Ge, organiser of the Guangdong New Image Slideshow Festival, came in for particular criticism for what was described as his "excessive" photographic exploration.

The rumble of controversy that accompanied these shows demonstrated the bafflement of many at these experimentations in new photography. It also highlighted fundamental differences between commentators in the north – by tradition instinctively more conservative – and those in the ideologically more relaxed south regarding issues of ideology, the relationship between life and art, and approaches to creativity.

Despite such complaints, introspective, personal photography began to quickly gain ground, not only in Guangdong but also further afield in China's other urban centres. In 2002, the curator Zeng Han organized the photography show Invisible City at Shanghai's Starlight Gallery displaying the works of 15 photographers.

In the same year in Shanghai, Zeng Yicheng, one of the most representative photographers from the south held the exhibition We Still Haven't Travelled Hand In Hand at Origin Gallery. The works narrated a personal love story that, among other things, sought to break the conventional reportage format of photography and explore new elements such as expression driven by emotion. On the whole Zeng's exhibition maintained traditional photographic integrity and even a classic quality, yet subsequent photographers clearly felt no need for this. As a result, personal photography began to move closer to contemporary art in its concerns and format.

Still another important reason for the rise of personal photography is its close relationship with the city. In their exploration of China's changing urban landscape many photographers – especially those in Shanghai and Guangdong – have unexpectedly discovered that topics from daily life cannot be avoided. Consequently, many have increasingly turned their work towards their own lives. Ya Niu, from Guangdong photographed himself everyday for one year, becoming the subject of a close, long-term examination. Elsewhere, in Shanghai Nights, Shanghai-based Yao Songxin created a series that began with evening scenes of the city's street corners and gradually evolved into scenes from the photographer's own love life. Meanwhile in Love's Touch /Caress, Yao reveals his emotions gradually over a series of self-portraits, turning the project into a poem based on his own life.

While the popularity of photography as a form of self expression has grown, the support of some sections of the popular media has also had an important effect on promoting the aesthetics and ideas of the personal photography movement. In particular, the immense influence of Guangzhou's City Pictorial magazine in advocating personal photography cannot be easily overlooked, even if its support is not without some consideration of its young target audience.

The magazine's most important issue was a special edition entitled Photographic Personal Life[1], which presented photography and personal life as related topics. This special edition came with two sections. The first was entitled China's Vanguard of Personal Photography and featured the work of Yao Songxin, Lin Zhi Peng (known online as 223), Bai Chuan and Tang Xiaoshuang, among others. The inclusion of photography enthusiast and movie actress Zhou Xun only seemed to underline the growing "coolness" of the new movement.

The second section was called Foreign Masters of Personal Photography and featured such high profile figures as Nobuyashi Araki, Wolfgang Tillmans, Sally Mann, Nan Goldin and Terry Richardson. The magazine identified the group as having established a link between photography and an expression of self identity. In its lead article it praised the new style of photography as providing a sort of "glue" for communities of relationships between people. The final statement from the magazine's Letter to Readers quoted the photographer Zeng Han: "Pick up your cameras. Photography is your personal life; your personal life is photography!"[2]

Such enthusiasm found solid form the same year when Zeng Han took the idea of "selfishness" as the inspiration for a group exhibition he curated at the Lianzhou Photography Festival in 2005 entitled Self, Personal. The exhibition was later combined with a group exhibition called Absent Minded, organised by Shanghai-based curator Shi Hantao, for a show in Guangzhou. Together, the two exhibitions provide a roll call of some of the leading figures in the personal photography movement, most of who are still in their 20s. In the exhibition catalogue, Zeng for the first time uses the phrase "New Generation Photographers", later identifying the function of photography and art in society as a way for individuals to "describe their own existence and to confirm their self-worth."[3]

The Super 80's (EpSITE New Imaging Gallery, Shanghai, April 2006) exhibition was yet another milestone and an important contribution to definitions of the new generation of photographers born in the 1980s.

The exhibition was based on the Super 1980's special edition of City Pictorial[4], which presented 80 portraits of young people born in that decade, each of them shown in their bedroom surrounded by possessions. The project, shot by City Pictorial staff, provided a seamless transition from magazine to exhibition format as well as a fascinating glimpse inside the lives of a broad range of young people in China. As magazine editor Gui Mei commented, "Their most valued secret is the bedroom self."[5]

In their private space, each sitter reveals an unrestrained persona while simultaneously highlighting a relationship with the camera that is completely different from their parent's generation. While their parent's might have considered having one's photograph taken as a kind of ritual, here the relationship is less rigid and the sitters appear comfortable expressing themselves naturally before the camera. This exhibit indicates a generation at ease with the photographic medium and can even be considered as a symbolic representation of their collective identity. Although the title First Generation Photographers is no longer sufficient to describe the generation born in the 1980s, one thing is certain: photography is a natural and even necessary element of their lives.

Lastly, it can also be seen that far from merely reporting New Generation Photography, the mass media is also active in guiding its production through the creation of trends with intergenerational appeal and room for self-expression. In other words, mass media has already begun to directly influence the cultural production of society.

1. City Pictorial (城市画报), 2005 Issue 16
2. City Pictorial (城市画报), 2005 Issue 16, p. 39
3. Zeng Han, Self, Personal, exhibition catalogue, 2005, Guangzhou, p. 2
4. City Pictorial (城市画报), 2006 Issue 5
5. City Pictorial (城市画报), 2006 Issue 5, p. 61

Narratives of New Generation Photography tend to be at least partially autobiographical. Even so, they express a collective visual expression and speak on behalf of shared values and existence using a variety of channels that include the Internet, gallery exhibitions, books and magazines, among others. The narratives function as a medium for mutual identification between the self and the other, where a person can discover people who hold similar values, establish their own values and express their individualism.

For example, Shanghai-based photographer Liu Yi Qing (Yiki) uses photography as a chance to assume the roles of individuals from different Asian cultures. Liu first received acclaim for her photography on the Internet before finally emerging on to the gallery circuit. She has since gone on to hold numerous full-scale exhibitions both in China and overseas. Liu provides only one example of the power of the Internet. Similarly, Lin Zhi Peng (223) first garnered online acclaim before moving beyond the virtual space to straddle both online as well as offline practices.

Although their works vary quite considerably, both are bonded by a common disregard for organized authority and are content to belong within a community of like-minded members. Ironically, although online communities can serve to alienate urban dwellers and impose barriers to "real" interaction, the great benefit of the Internet is that such virtual communities invite participation from a potentially huge audience spread out across China and even including other countries. The flip side to this are the very fragile connections that often hold these communities together, which in many cases do not extend much further than members' own feelings of social alienation.

The piece Birdhead World 2004-2005 by Shanghai-based Song Tao and Xiao Ji (also Ji Wei Yu) features the artists photographing each other and various street-level detritus in dozens of deliberately un-picturesque urban locations. Aside from the bleak backgrounds and litter, the works frequently focus on the artists themselves. The photographic medium allows them to express a unique dual identity and the work almost assumes the status of a performance documented.

From this perspective Guangdong photographer Bai Chuan's piece, Perhaps Bamboo, displays the same subtleties as Birdhead but uses a different approach. In Perhaps Bamboo, Bai photographs the daily life of a friend in an attempt to use the narrowest field of vision to reflect the most symbolic realities of private life.

In both pieces, the photographers highlight two important common qualities in the work of many new generation photographers: first, their determination not to be regulated or restrained in any way; and second, their creation of a highly focused dialogue that excludes wider social contact. In effect, the works exist within small communities and the photographers do not seek to engage with the world outside until the outside world reaches out to them. Thus, these photographers are not exposed to photography through society, but rather to society through photography. By using this technique new generation photographers also tend to create a magnified or altered idea of the self in order to make a statement. As a result, photography becomes important for nurturing and glorifying individualism. Perhaps Lin Zhi Peng's declaration, "I am an irresponsible person" is the most succinct expression of this.

Lin professes: "When I photograph, I don't use the methods of documentary or realistic expression. I merely use the lens in place of real life. Sometimes I photograph my own life; sometimes I snap private photographs of nearby people, objects and things. Everyone who replaces real life with the camera is the same."

Lin refuses to use his photography to differentiate between his own ambitions and the ambitions of others. While photography of this kind might produce images indistinguishable from those of a casual photographer, a fundamental contrast remains where meticulous organization and editing of the images is used to reveal a unique identity.

Through the use of this process photography can assume the status of a personal "literary" form. In a reality saturated with private dialogues, these photographers seek a special vocabulary for speaking to the heart. They craft a personalised photographic grammar for dialoguing with the self and in many cases it is the city that becomes the ultimate arena for providing inspiration and material. Shanghai photographer Dai Mouyu captures extraordinary colours in his works that attempt to express the idea of isolation within the city. People are suffused with bright colours that reflect their thoughts and desires. Dai's images magnify the strangeness and inexplicability of the metropolis. In particular, the photographs taken between midnight and dawn expose the city as a wilderness, awash in fragmented colours and the poetics of weariness and alienation. This type of work rejects references and narrative and an analysis of its form reflects a fragmentation of the society it seeks to portray.

6. Zeng Han, Self, Personal, exhibition catalogue, 2005, Guangzhou, p.69

It is not easy to define personal photography. A narrow definition might be private photography, yet in a broader sense personal photography might extend beyond the realms of the family and self-portraiture to include photographs of whatever crosses one's path. Moreover, an expression of individualism in a photographic practice does not necessarily render it "personal photography". And while the camera lens may be directed towards the photographer's own life, or life within a very exclusive community, personal photography in the artistic sense seeks to make public something that is usually non-accessible, often to a wide and unknown audience.

The personal life mentioned here does not refer to the traditional notion of family life. Instead, the subject of personal photography might entail a specific phase in an individual's life or in the life of a tight-knit community. In addition, the relationship between the photographer and the photographed is based on mutual values and life attitudes. Each has a mutual understanding and tacitly approves of the existence of a camera within personal space. Thus, due to this existent mutual interaction the images can sometimes display the qualities of a live performance. These photographers do not seek the approval of the mainstream media but ask only that they can express their own views. Very often it is the Internet that provides the channel for this.

This opening up of Chinese society's consumer revolution marks a period of immense transition in which values and standards are constantly redefined. As a consequence, young people in China have the opportunity to create a new social discourse, using both the resources at hand, such as photography, the Internet and other new technology, as well as the support of certain sections of mass media. These individuals are not the products of "popular" opinion and mass media but are directly influenced by the ideology of the individual and concepts of the personal. They play a necessary and powerful role in the cultural production and formation of a consumer society and their efforts have weakened the social influence of mainstream ideology. Of course, whether or not they have merely replaced one ideology with another needs further investigation. Yet it is obvious that they are no longer willing to submit themselves to mainstream opinion and authority.

One result of the popularity of photography and its presence in the personal life is a change in the relationship between public space and private space. Barthes said: "The era of photography coincides with the era in which private life emerges in the public arena. Or perhaps it is identical to creating an era of new social values dominated by the public consumption of the private."

Increasingly, a photographer first receives online acclaim that garners interest and then moves through the gallery and festival circuit along a path that invariably leads to the market. The link between personal photography and all kinds of public consumption has become much more direct. In China, factors such as social, political and economic development have delayed the popularization of photography, yet the pattern of events in China mirrors that of a capitalist consumer society. With regards to so-called "Chinese personal photography", the important question is how to reconstruct the concept of "I" to incorporate new concepts of "public" and "private", while still retaining personal feelings and perceptions."[8]

Personal photography rejects grand narratives and avoids making judgments. The challenge is preserving the strength to react. From the perspective of contemporary photography abroad, the personal is not necessarily separate from the social. One of the main problems facing contemporary Chinese photography is the growing imbalance between individual perceptions on the one hand and creating a more engaged relationship between the self and society on the other.

Yet another problem that is rapidly gaining attention is the monotony of technique. Sometimes garish exhibition arrangements are employed to compensate for this and on occasion the result is inconsequence or narcissism. Personal photography needs to evolve to express something that is useful to society or face its demise.

The emergence and development of Chinese personal photography is not an isolated cultural phenomenon. It is an important and necessary phase in the cultural development of a society undergoing political and economic transformation. Such a transition brings with it immense potential, as different fields, structures and powers act upon and remake each other. Although we already have a good grasp of the beneficial traits and are at the fore of the trend, regardless, a style of personal photography that is a cultural disposition is already sufficient for us to think anew about the relationship between photography and reality in order to reach a broader reflection of truth. From some points of view personal photography is no longer the exclusive concern of photographers.

Translated by Philana Woo

7. Barthes, Roland, Howard, Richard (trans.),
   Camera Lucida: Reflections on Photography, Hill and Wang, 1981,
   New York, p. 98
8. Ibid., p. 98

The Guangdong-Hong Kong Information Daily[1] first appeared in 1993. It quickly became known for its weekend supplement that featured lifestyle articles on subjects that the mainstream news press had mostly ignored up to that point. It had a huge appetite for alternative content and it was here that my first articles were published. It was also at this time that Shen Hao joined Southern Weekend[2] magazine. Under Shen, the magazine revamped its editorial style and became part of a wider revolution taking place in the Guangzhou mass media. Where previously TV and the press had served only as mouthpieces for government propaganda, now, suddenly, the industry was thrown open to the market. This and the heady spirit of freedom of expression that it seemed to promise attracted many young people to the industry, whether as full-time staff or as freelancers. Without doubt it was an exceptional moment to be involved in the media in China.

As these changes rippled outwards, the Pearl River Delta, with Guangzhou at its centre, gained a reputation as a region unafraid to strike out on its own. The city's close proximity to the then British Crown Colony of Hong Kong was an important factor. The tiny colony had been a refuge for reformers since the 19th century and temporary residents had included the scholar and exile Kang You Wei, who had visited the city in 1879 and was impressed by its clean streets and efficient social system. Other notable reformers to have spent time in the colony include the father of the modern republic, Dr Sun Yat Sen.

The Canadian media theorist Marshall McLuhan believed that the market is the premise of democracy and the development of Guangzhou's media industry in the early 1990s seemed to confirm this. There is perhaps significance in the fact that in the Chinese name for Southern Weekend (pronounced "Nan Fang Zhou Mo"), "Nang Fang", which means south, is also a synonym for reform and carries the idea of "brave to be the first".

As a result, it is interesting to speculate on how the development of China might have been different had Deng Xiaoping not toured the region in 1992 to re-focus the course of reform in the Shenzhen Special Economic Zone – particularly with the bloodshed of June 4, 1989, still fresh in people's memories.

Yet even the introduction of measured changes had a dramatic effect on Guangzhou's media industry. The need to attract more advertisers and readers caused many publications to expand their content and adopt a more powerful visual style. In pushing out their boundaries many also opened their doors to young media professionals and graduates – the kinds of people whose ideas had previously been overlooked. In the ensuing decade numerous young photographers in southern China emerged whose work reflects the influence of their day jobs in the media, from the high-gloss of fashion magazines to the gritty aesthetic of street-side photography.

One of the most influential of these publications was Focus magazine[3]. The publication had previously been entitled Modern Photography[4], but by the 1980s, under its chief editor Li Mei it had changed its name and expanded its content to include reportage and general human interest stories. It had also successfully nurtured a band of photographers who were keen to produce images of "New China" and key among these was the documentary photographer An Ge.

From his base in Guangzhou An travelled all over the country to record the daily life of people during the Deng era. His works

are characterised by their human scale and today make up a rich social history of China in the late 20th century. His long engagement with the medium and commitment to his subject also established him as a role model for many young photographers such as Yan Chang Jiang, Wang Ning De, and A Niu.

Another influential publication was New Weekly magazine[5], which was founded in Guangzhou in 1996. Its principal photographer was Zhang Hai Er who was already well-known for his experimental black and white images that focused on the absurdities of daily urban living. After joining New Weekly Zhang began to introduce colour and a new range of subjects to his work. He was not interested in examining historic particulars and social messages but instead focused on moments of fleeting reality. His portraits are tightly framed to de-contextualise the subject and emphasise the sitter's gaze, as if attempting to peer into their soul. Today, Zhang remains one of China's most distinguished urban photographers whose works pierce the heart of the city. His photographic style has also had an important impact on a number of young generation photographers including Chen Ying Yu, Zeng Yi Cheng, Ma Ling and Zeng Han, who in the latter 1990s were working for such magazines as City Pictorial[6] and Southern Metropolitan Daily[7].

1. Guangdong-Hong Kong Information Daily (粤港信息时报)
2. Southern Weekend (南方周末)
3. Focus (现代摄影)
4. Modern Photography (现代摄影)
5. New Weekly Magazine (新周刊)
6. City Pictorial (城市画报)
7. Southern Metropolitan Daily (南方都市报)

Of all Guangzhou's magazines the fastest growing has been Modern Weekly[8]. The magazine was revamped in 1998 to appeal to an urban, white-collar readership. Today its format lies somewhere between a magazine and a tabloid newspaper. Dramatic photos instantly draw the eye and since 2000 it has built a reputation for its edgy articles and collaborations with a number of well-known artists, including Cao Fei, who showed her first series of works, Games (2000) and Collection Boxes (2001) in the magazine.

Cao is by far the best known of the young generation photographers to have emerged from the Guangzhou media scene. In addition to Modern Weekly, Cao's works have appeared in several city publications. She debuted her Freshness series – a homage to Shuji Terayama and David LaChapelle – in Phoenix Weekly[9] in 2002. Yet it is the Cosplayer series for which she is best known. The series was originally created as part of a video piece of the same name and unlike previous works, which were photographed in a studio, it was shot at different locations around Guangzhou. In so doing she acknowledges the influence of Ye Jianqiang, a photographer at Guangzhou Evening News,[10] whose taste for Guangzhou's raw street life she shares.

In her photography and videos Cao offers an artistic vision of the city; its folk histories and legends as well as its social problems. Yet she is distinct from the preceding generation of photographers in her frequent references to popular culture, particularly that of Hong Kong, Taiwan, Japan and Korea, to which she adds a direct, no-nonsense approach. As a result Cao's works point ahead to a new generation of artist-photographers who are only now beginning to emerge.

In particular, the Internet has shown its importance as an economically viable platform for emerging urban youth subcultures. Young photographers can work for the traditional print media during the day and create their own online visual paradises at night. So Han Guang (known online as Alex) is a photographer for Seen[11] magazine and founder of the e-zine Coldtea[12]. His ability to capture a raw, authentic feel in his portraits of narcissistic teenagers gives the magazine its distinctive feel and has proved so popular that a spin-off e-zine called After 17[13] was recently launched.

Such projects illustrate the need felt by China's emerging generation for a voice that is distinct from the mainstream media. The Internet provides a space for this at a low cost as well as the opportunity to contact other like-minded individuals. In this way Lin Zhi Peng (223) is typical of such artists. In addition to being a photographer for the Guangzhou-based print magazine Hua Xia Wen Zhai,[14] he has gained notoriety for his photo blog[15]. Lin's works typically have a rough-and-ready feel in which photographic technique is frequently neglected for the sake of compelling immediacy. His subjects seem content to reject all responsibility in pursuit of all-night parties and fashionable indolence. A clear inspiration can be found in the work of Juergen Teller and Terry Richardson, both freelance photographers for UK-based I-D Magazine. Similar feelings of social alienation can be found in the work of magazine photographer Yang Chang Hong whose blurry, unfocused images feel like abstract experiments in colours and shape.

Today, the media industry in Guangzhou remains an important focus for new photography in China, both as a champion of new work and a breeding ground for emerging talent. And as their ideas spread and are taken up by photographers in China's other cities, new notions of identity and creativity are being created to fit a different set of aspirations.

Translated by Phoebe Wong

8. Modern Weekly (周末画报)

9. Phoenix Weekly (凤凰周刊)

10. Guangzhou Evening News (羊城晚报)

11. Seen magazine (香港风情)

12. www.coldtea.cn (凉茶)

13. www.after17magazine.com

14. Hua Xia Wen Zhai (华夏)

15. www.blogcn.com/user4/finger_blue/index.html

BIRDHEAD 鸟头

JI WEI YU 季 炜煜　　　SONG TAO 宋 涛

1980	Born in Shanghai
1996-2000	Shanghai College of Arts and Crafts (Graphic Design)
2000-2004	Central Saint Martins College of Art and Design (Graphic Design)
2004	Co-founder, Birdhead
	Lives in Shanghai
	www.birdheadworld.com

1979	Born in Shanghai
1995-1998	Shanghai College of Arts and Crafts
2004	Co-founder, Birdhead
	Lives in Shanghai
	www.birdheadworld.com

Selected Group Exhibitions

2006　Restless: Photography and New Media, Museum of Contemporary Art, Shanghai, China

2005　Birdhead World 2004-2005: Photography by Song Tao & Ji Wei Yu, Shanghart Gallery, Shanghai, China

Solo Exhibitions

2006　Ya Cinema, temporary venue, Shanghai, China

2003　A Kind of Format, BizArt Center, Shanghai, China

2001　Song Tao Solo Exhibition – The Floor, Shanghart Gallery, Shanghai, China

1999　The Last Five Minutes of the 20th Century, Eastlink Gallery, Shanghai, China

Selected Group Exhibitions

2006　Restless: Photography and New Media, Museum of Contemporary Art, Shanghai, China

2006　China Contemporary, Architecture, Art & Visual Culture, Netherlands Architecture Institute Museum, Boijmans Van Beuningen, Netherlands Fotomuseum, the Netherlands

2005　Birdhead World 2004-2005: Photography by Song Tao & Ji Wei Yu, Shanghart Gallery, Shanghai, China

'05 4 25

Birdhead World 2004-2005 series

CAI WEI DONG 蔡 卫东

1978   Born in Tianshui, Gansu Province
1998-2002   Beijing Film Academy
Lives in Beijing

Selected Group Exhibitions

2006   Uncertain Expression, Zero Field Experimental Art Center, Beijing, China
2006   Secular Life, Song Zhong Art Cooperative Society of Beijing, China
2005   Guangzhou Photography Biennial, Guangdong Museum of Art, Guangzhou, China
2005   Pingyao International Photography Festival, Pingyao, China
2005   10th Song Zhong Invitational Exhibition, Beijing Song Zhong Art Village, Beijing, China

▲ Landscape (details), 2000-2004
◄◄ My Back, 2005

Landscape, 2000-2004

CAO FEI 曹 斐

1978   Born in Guangzhou, Guangdong Province
1997-2001   Guangzhou Academy of Fine Arts
Lives in Beijing
www.caofei.com

Solo Exhibitions

2006   What Are You Doing Here? Siemens Art Program,
        OSRAM China Lighting Ltd., Foshan, China
2006   Hip-Hop, Lombard-Freid Projects, New York, USA
2005   Cosplayers, Lombard-Freid Fine Arts, New York, USA
2005   Cosplayers, Courtyard Gallery, Beijing, China
2004   San Yuan Li, Courtyard Gallery, Beijing, China

Selected Group Exhibitions

2006   15th Biennale of Sydney, Sydney, Australia
2005   A Kind of Portraiture, Art Basel Miami Beach
        Art Video Lounge, USA
2005   Exchange Value of Pleasure, Busan Museum of
        Modern Art, South Korea
2005   Second Guangzhou Triennial: Beyond – An Extraordinary
        Space of Experimentation for Modernization,
        Guangdong Museum of Art, Guangzhou, China
2005   Tirana Biennale, National Gallery of Arts, Tirana, Albania
2005   Trouble with Fantasy, Kunsthalle Nurnberg, Nurnberg,
        Germany
2005   Out of Sight, De Appel Foundation of Amsterdam,
        the Netherlands
2005   Third Fukuoka Asian Art Triennial: Parallel Realities – Asian
        Art Now, Fukuoka Asian Art Museum, Japan
2005   Follow Me! Contemporary Chinese Art at the Threshold of
        the Millennium, Mori Museum, Tokyo, Japan
2005   China! China!! China!!! Grace Alexander Contemporary
        Art Gallery, Zurich, Switzerland

2005   I Still Believe in Miracles Part II: Derrière l' horizon,
        Musee d' Art moderne de la Ville de Paris, France
2005   Emergency Biennale in Chechnya: A Suitcase from Paris to Grosny,
        Palais de Tokyo, Paris, France
2005   First Moscow Biennale of Contemporary Art: Dialectics of Hope,
        Moscow, Russia
2005   Water Event, Yoko Ono - Horizontal Memories,
        Astrup Fearnley Museum of Modern Art, Oslo, Norway
2005   London + China Film Festival 2005, School of Oriental and
        African Studies, University of London, UK
2004   Past in Reverse: Contemporary Art of East Asia,
        San Diego Museum of Art, USA
2004   Die Chinesen: Fotografie und Video aus China,
        Kunstmuseum Wolfsburg, Germany
2004   Fifth Shanghai Biennale: Techniques of the Visible,
        Shanghai Art Museum, China
2004   Between Past and Future: New Photography and Video from
        China, International Center of Photography and Asia Society,
        New York, USA (touring exhibition)
2004   China Now, Museum of Modern Art Film at
        the Gramercy Theater, New York, USA
2004   Chine: Génération Video, Maison Européenne de la Photographie,
        Paris, France
2004   Out the Window: Spaces of Distraction, Japan Foundation
        Asia Center, Tokyo, Japan
2003   10th Biennial of the Moving Image, Centre pour l' image
        Contemporaine, Geneva, Switzerland

Tussle, 2004

A Hutong War, 2006

▲ Nada at Home, 2004
▶ Hello! Kitty, 2006
▶ Erector's Sword, 2006

Housebreaker, 2006

Old Wu Kong, 2006

CHEN WEI 陈 维

1980   Born in Shanghai

Lives in Hangzhou, Zhejiang Province

Selected Group Exhibitions

2006   Poetic Reality: A Reinterpretation of Jiangnan, RCM Art Museum, Nanjing, China

2006   Restless: Photography and New Media, Museum of Contemporary Art, Shanghai, China

2005   GIFT, Museum of Modern Art, Hangzhou Teachers College, China

2004   Bai Ta Ling, temporary venue, Hangzhou, China

2003   TomeClub Version 2, temporary venue, Hangzhou, China

Performances

2005   2pi Festival 2005, temporary venues, Hangzhou, China

2005   Four Seasons Tour, temporary venue, Shanghai/Beijing, China

2005   Chu Shen (12-hour Audio-Visual Performance), temporary venue, Shanghai, China

2004   2pi Festival 2004, temporary venues, Hangzhou, China

2004   Domestic Violence #2, temporary venue, Hangzhou, China

2003   2pi Festival 2003, temporary venues, Hangzhou, China

▲ Countless Unpredictable Stand 3, 2006
▶▶ Countless Unpredictable Stand 1, 2006

Countless Unpredictable Stand 5, 2006

▲ Countless Unpredictable Stand 2, 2006
▼ Countless Unpredictable Stand 4, 2006

CHI PENG 迟 鹏

1981   Born in Yantai, Shandong Province
2001-2005   Central Academy of Fine Arts, Beijing
Lives in Beijing

Solo Exhibitions

2006   Up, White Space Beijing, China
2005   Naked Lunch, Chambers Fine Art, New York, USA

Selected Group Exhibitions

2006   China Avantgarde, Wiedergeburt des Mystischen, Museum Klosterneuburg
        Sammlung Essl, Vienna, Austria
2006   Signs of Existence, Central Academy of Fine Arts Gallery Beijing, China
2006   The Sacred and the Profane, Alexander Ochs Galleries Berlin/Beijing, Germany
2006   Palmbeach3, Alexander Ochs Galleries Berlin/Beijing, USA
2006   Bitmap Opening: International Digital Photo 001, Seoul, South Korea
2005   Karlsruhe Barcelona Cambridge Toronto, Centre Georges Pompidou, Paris, France
2005   Asia: The Place To Be? Alexander Ochs Galleries Berlin/Beijing, Germany
2005   The Second Reality: Photographs From China, temporary venue, Brussels, Belgium
2005   Third Fukuoka Asian Art Triennial: Parallel Realities – Asian Art Now, Fukuoka
        Asian Art Museum, Japan
2005   Techno-Orientalism, Beijing Tokyo Art Project, Beijing, China
2005   Ber Schönheit, Haus der Kulturen der Welt, Berlin, Germany
2005   Beauty Berlin, Alexander Ochs Galleries Berlin/Beijing, Germany
2005   Performance the Body: Contemporary Photography from China, Alexander Ochs
        Galleries Berlin/Beijing, Germany
2005   Body Scape, ARC One Gallery, Melbourne, Australia
2005   Body Temperature: Invoking the Legacy of Hans Christian Anderson through
        Chinese Contemporary Art, Nordjyllands Kunstmuseum, Denmark and Beijing Millennium
        Art Museum, Beijing, China
2005   Chinese Photography Today, Chambers Fine Art, New York, USA
2004   Touch, Central Academy of Fine Arts Gallery, Beijing, China
2004   Visual Gallery at Photokina, Cologne, Germany (touring exhibition)
2004   One to One: Recent Photographs from China, Chambers Fine Art,
        New York, USA

▲ I Fuck Me - Bathroom, 2005
◄◄ I Fuck Me - Public Toilet, 2005

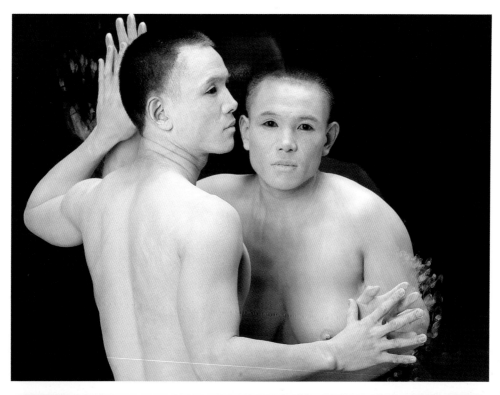

▲ Consubstantiality-1-1, 2003
▼ Consubstantiality-1-2, 2003

Mirage, 2005

GUO HANG 郭 航

1983   Born in Taiyuan, Shanxi Province
2002-2006   Central Academy of Fine Arts, Beijing
Lives in Beijing

Selected Group Exhibitions

2006   China Dreaming, Southwark Underground Station, London, UK
2006   Object France, Centre Culturel Français de Pekin, Beijing, China

▲ Family - Grandfather, 2005

◄◄ Family - Aunt, 2005

▲ Family - Uncle, 2005   ▲ Family - Mother, 2005

▼ Family - Cousin 1, 2005   ▼ Family - Cousin 2, 2005

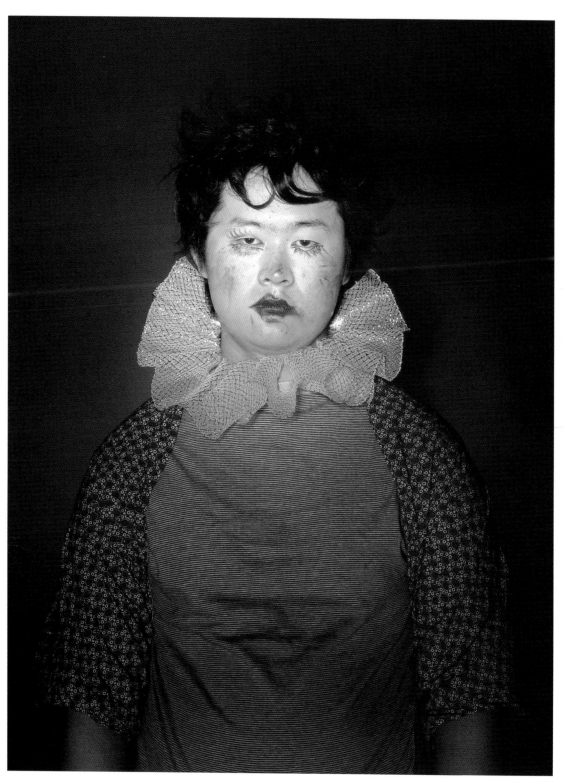

Doll 5, 2006

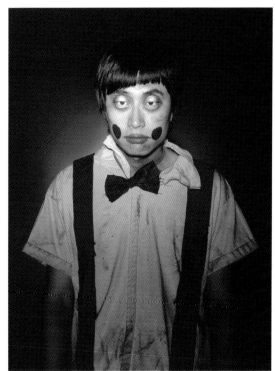

◄ Doll 6, 2006
► Doll 7, 2006

HUANG KUI 黄 奎

1977   Born in Renshou, Sichuan Province
1996-2000   Sichuan Fine Art College (Oil Painting)
Lives in Shanghai

Solo Exhibitions

2006   VIP, temporary venue, Shanghai, China

Selected Group Exhibitions

2006   Sixth Shanghai Biennale: Hyper Design, Shanghai Art Museum, China
2006   Migration Addicts 2, temporary venue, Singapore
2006   Contemporary Video from Asia, Bonhams 1793, London, UK
2006   Exposition d'Art Contemporain de Shanghai, La Grande Arche de la Défense, Paris, France
2006   Restless: Photography and New Media, Museum of Contemporary Art, Shanghai, China
2005   Conspire, Beijing TS1 Contemporary Art Center, Beijing, China
2005   Asian Traffic, temporary venue, Shanghai, China
2005   Rumor Décor, DDM Warehouse, Shanghai, China
2005   6 Wigwams, temporary venue, Shanghai, China
2005   Inward Gazes: Documentaries of Chinese Performance Art, temporary venue,
        Macao SAR, China
2005   920 Kilograms, Shanghai Duolun Museum of Modern Art, China
2005   China Contemporary Performance Art – Video & Photography, Taipei, Taiwan
2005   Back to the Future - Shanghai Art, temporary venue, Germany/ Poland
2005   Migration Addicts, temporary venue, Shanghai, China
2004   Black & White, temporary venue, Shanghai, China
2004   Young Artists Exhibition, Shanghai Duolun Museum of Modern Art, Shanghai, China
2004   62761232: Express Delivery Contemporary Art (Express delivery to destinations in Shanghai)
2003   Electrolyte, Nanjing Shenghua Art Center, China
2002   Mushroom or Utopia, temporary venue, Shanghai, China
2002   Daydream, temporary venue, Nanjing, China
2002   It's Begun, temporary venue, Shanghai, China
2002   Feel the Spot, temporary venue, Guangxi, China
2002   N-ply Identity, temporary venue, Nanjing, China
2001   Parabola, temporary venue, Chengdu, China
2001   Chinese Project 360°, Sea and Mountain Art Centre, Shanghai, China
2000   Wondering in the Language, temporary venue, Chongqing, China
1999   He She You and I, temporary venue, Chongqing, China

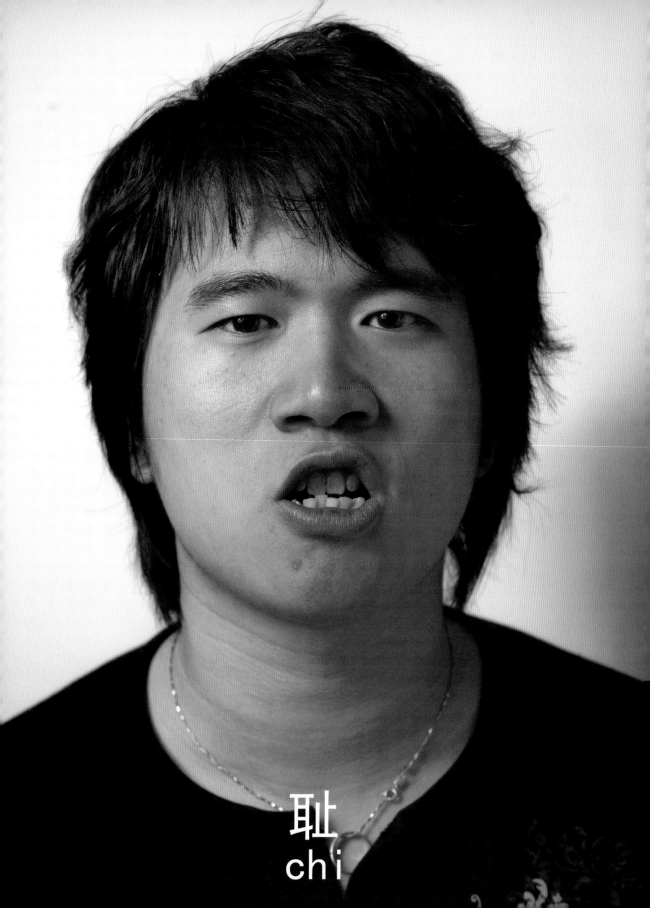

耻
chi

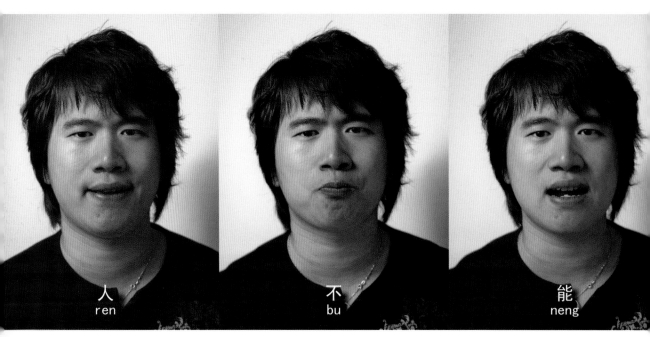

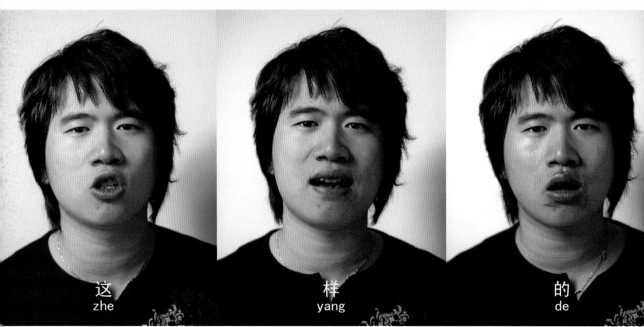

◄◄ A Man Shall Not Be So Shameless, 2006 (detail)

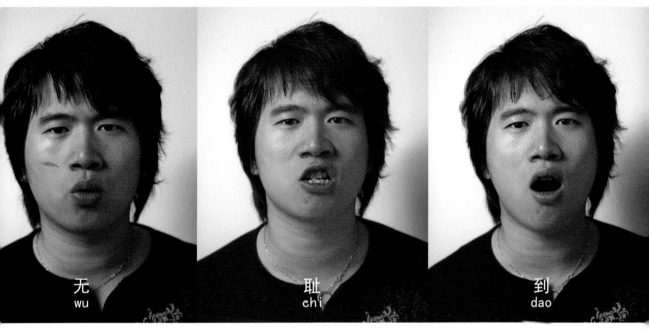

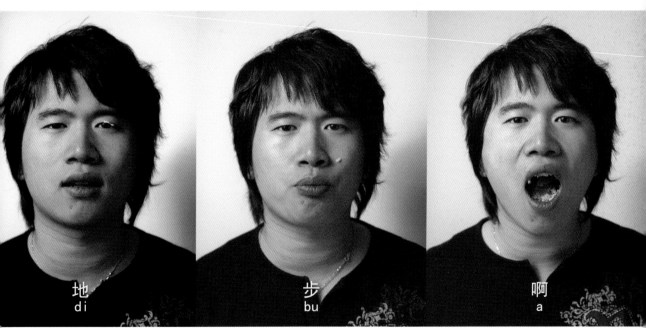

A Man Shall Not Be So Shameless, 2006

JIN SHAN 金 闪

1976   Born in Tonglu, Zhejiang Province
2003-2006   China University of Geosciences, Beijing
Lives in Hangzhou

Selected Group Exhibitions

2006   Fourth Seoul International Media Art Biennale, Seoul Museum of Art, South Korea
2006   Flight Log: Third China Independent Film Festival, Nanjing, China
2006   Restless: Photography and New Media, Museum of Contemporary Art,
        Shanghai, China
2006   Frequency Post, Kunstradio, Vienna, Austria
2005   GIFT, Museum of Modern Art, Hangzhou Teachers College, China
2004   Bai Ta Lin, temporary venue, Hangzhou, China

▲ Fat Monkey #2, 2006
▶ Fat Monkey #3, 2006
◀◀ Fat Monkey #1, 2006

LI SI EN 李 思恩

1980   Born in Ruian, Zhejiang Province
2003-2004   China Academy of Art, Zhejiang (New Media)
Lives in Hangzhou
http://bne.blogbus.com/index.html

Selected Group Exhibitions

2006   China Qingse, Ag-Art Loft, Hangzhou, China
2004   Landscape, Loft 49, Hangzhou, China

Portrait series, 2006

Beach series, 2006

LIANG YUE 梁玥

1979   Born in Shanghai
1997-2001   Shanghai College of Fine Art
Lives in Shanghai

Solo Exhibitions

2005   Stop Dazing, BizArt Center, Shanghai, China
2004   Until the Morn, Galerie du Tableau, Marseille, France
2003   Several Dusks, Shanghart Gallery, Shanghai, China
2002   Don't Think About Anything, BizArt Center,
        Shanghai, China

Selected Group Exhibitions

2006   The Thirteen: Chinese Video Now, P.S.1 Contemporary
        Art Centre, New York, USA
2006   Move on Asia 2006, Alternative Space Loop, Seoul, South Korea
2006   Never Go Out Without My DV Cam: Video Art from China,
        Museo Colecciones ICO, Madrid, Spain
2006   Stop Dazing in Anthology, Film Archives, New York, USA
2006   Restless: Photography and New Media, Museum of
        Contemporary Art, Shanghai, China
2006   Twilight, Victoria & Albert Museum, London, UK
2005   Guangzhou Second Triennial: Beyond – An Extraordinary
        Space of Experimentation for Modernization:
        Guangdong Art Museum, Guangzhou, China
2005   F in Media, Alternative Space Loop, Seoul, South Korea
2004   China Now, Museum of Modern Art Film at the Gramercy Theater ,
        New York, USA
2004   Feverish Unconscious: Digital Culture in Contemporary China,
        Chambers Fine Art, New York, USA
2004   Conceptual Photography from the People's Republic of China,
        Museum of Contemporary Art, Denver, USA
2004   All Under Heaven, Museum of Contemporary Art Antwerp, Belgium
2004   Le Moine et le Demon, Musée d'Art Contemporain de Lyon,
        France
2004   Opening Studio, Gasworks Studios, London, UK

2004   China Change – China Present: Everyday Life, Co Gallery,
        Berlin, Germany
2004   Light As Fuck! Shanghai Assemblage 2000-2004, National Museum of
        Contemporary Art, Oslo, Norway
2004   Argosfestival, Brussels, Belgium.
2004   A l'ouest du sud de l'est, Centre Regional d'Art Contemporain
        Languedoc-Roussillon, Sete, France
2003   Open Sky, Shanghai Duolun Museum of Modern Art, China
2003   Urbanart2003, Melbourne, Australia
2003   Zooming into Focus: Chinese Contemporary Photography and Video
        from the Haudenschild Collection, San Diego State University and
        San Diego Museum of Art, San Diego, USA
2003   +System - Short Videos from the World 2002-2003, BizArt Center,
        Shanghai, China
2003   Chinese Maximalism, Millennium Art Museum, Beijing, China
2004   Chine: Génération Video, Maison Européene de la Photographie,
        Paris, France
2002   24:30, BizArt Center, Shanghai, China
2002   Fan Mingzhen & Fan Mingzhu – Glad to Meet, temporary venue,
        Shanghai, China
2001   Futi, temporary venue, Hangzhou, China
2001   Homeport - Fuxing Park, BizArt Center, Shanghai, China
2000   Uncooperative Approach (Fuck Off), Eastlink Gallery, Shanghai, China
1999   The Same But Also Changed, temporary venue, Shanghai

Morse Code, 2004

▲ Daylight Wakening a, 2005
▼ Daylight Wakening b, 2005
◄◄ Ionic, 2005

Liang Yue

Early Fall Rain, 2005

Morse Code series, 2004

LIN ZHI PENG (223) 林 志鹏

1979   Born in Guangzhou, Guangdong Province
1996-2000   Guangdong University of Foreign Studies
2004   Co-founder, Nature-Graphy Society, China
Lives in Guangzhou
www.blogcn.com/user4/finger_blue/index.html

Selected Group Exhibitions

2006   I, CHINA, Da Space, Shanghai, China
2006   Selfhood-Absent Minded: Joint Exhibition of New Generation
        Photographers in China, Guangzhou, China (touring exhibition)
2005   Game Zone City Lomo Photographic Week, Guangzhou, China
2005   Pingyao International Photography Festival, Pingyao, China

Publications

2006   United Nude, Milan International Future Exhibition, Milan, Italy

▲ Kiss, 2006
▶ Hair, 2006
◀◀ Hidden, 2006

▲ Afternoon with Blue Mood, 2006
▼ Spring Flower Girl, 2006
▶ Room, 2006

LIU BO 刘 波

1977   Born in Shishou, Hubei Province

1997-2001   Hubei Institute of Fine Arts (Oil Painting)

Lives in Wuhan

Selected Group Exhibitions

2005   920 Kilograms, Shanghai Duolun Museum of Modern Art, China

2005   Rumor Décor, DDM Warehouse, Shanghai, China

2005   What Are You Doing Here? Siemens Art Program 2005,
       Siemens Limited China, Wuhan, China

2004   Automatic Shopping Machine, Suzhou Art & Design Technology Institute, China

2004   Plug and Play, Wuhan Bai Zanting, China

2004   Next Station, Nanjing Shenghua Art Center, China

2004   Slowly, Wuhan Fine Arts Literature Art Center, China

2004   A Midsummer Night's Dream – The City in Phantasm, Wuhan Fine Arts
       Literature Art Center, China

2003   Electrolyte, Nanjing Shenghua Art Center, China

2002   New Urban Theory, Guangdong Museum of Art, Guangzhou, China

▲ Chimneys - Guan Shan Thermal Power Plant, Wuhan, 2006
▼ Water Towers - Central Chinese Normal University, 2006

▲ A burned body found in a building site, Guan Shan, Xiongchu Street, 2006

▼ Footmouse, 2006

Chongqing monk goes on a pilgrimage to Wuhan Guiyuan Temple, 2006

Follow you and sleep in your bed, 2006

LIU DING 刘 鼎

1976   Born in Changzhou, Jiangsu Province
2001   Founder, Pink Studio, Nanjing
2005   Co-founder, Complete Art Experience Project, Beijing
Lives in Beijing
http://blog.sina.com.cn/u/1220053071

Solo Exhibitions

2006   Samples from the Transition – Products, L.A.Galerie, Frankfurt,
       Germany
2006   Noah's Living Room – The Power of the Mass, Dartington College of Arts,
       UK
2005   Samples from the Transition – Treasure (installation project), Beijing Long
       March Project Room, Beijing, China
2004   Noah's Living Room – The Power of the Mass, China Unlimited, Berlin,
       Germany
2004   Image Beyond Image, Rooseum Test Site, Malmö, Sweden
2001   White Ecstasy (installation), Kayi Gallery, Nanjing, China
1998   Unbalance, Feifan Art Center, Nanjing, China

Selected Group Exhibitions

2006   The Amber Room, Luggage Store Gallery, San Francisco, USA
2006   Fourth Seoul International Media Art Biennale, Seoul Museum of Art,
       South Korea
2006   Chinese Contemporary Art Festival, Heyri Art Village, Seoul, South Korea
2006   Poetic Reality: A Reinterpretation of Jiangnan, RCM Art Museum,
       Nanjing, China
2006   Fancy - Dream, Marella Gallery, Beijing, China
       (touring exhibition)
2006   Long March Capital, Long March Space, Beijing, China
2006   Fiction@Love, Museum of Contemporary Art, Shanghai, China
2005   Renovation - Relations of Production, Long March Space, Beijing, China
2005   Ten Eras Ten Colors, Soka Contemporary Space, Beijing, China
2005   Second Guangzhou Triennial: Beyond – An Extraordinary Space of
       Experimentation for Modernization, Guangdong Art Museum,
       Guangzhou, China
2005   China-Green, Ag-Art Loft, Hangzhou, China
2005   Complete Art Experience Project No. 6: Playground of Authorship,
       University of Rochester, New York, USA
2005   Limitation and Freedom - Autumn Market, Wuhan Art Archives and
       Center, China

2005   Complete Art Experience Project No. 5 – 24 Hours, Beijing Film
       Studio, Beijing, China
2005   Archaeology of the Future: Second Triennial of Chinese Art,
       Nanjing Museum, China
2005   Complete Art Experience Project No. 1 – Incest, Platform China,
       Beijing, China
2005   In and Out or In-between – N Kinds of Space Displacement,
       Soka Contemporary Space, Beijing, China
2005   Reflections on the Everyday, L.A.Galerie, Frankfurt, Germany
2004   Undercurrents - Video from China, China Unlimited,
       Berlin, Germany
2004   55th Fondazione Premio Michetti Prize: Myth and Reality - A Look
       Towards the East, Michetti Museum, Francavilla al Mare, Italy
2004   Temporality, LA Gallery, Beijing, China
2004   Object System: Doing Nothing, ARCO Art Fair, Madrid, Spain

Further Information

2006   Artist in residence, Dartington College of Arts, UK
2005   Set design, Strindberg Love Letter, People's Art Theatre, Beijing,
       China
2004   Guest lecturer, Royal Academy of Fine Arts, Stockholm, Sweden

▲ Five Objects, 2002
◄ Timer, 2004
► Chinese Mushroom, 2003
◄◄ Timer, 2004 (detail)

◄ Globe, 2004
►► Untitled, 2001 (four photographs)

LIU REN 刘 韧

1980   Born in Qin Huangdao, Hebei Province
1997-2001   Yanshan University (Industrial Design)
2004-present   Central Academy of Fine Arts, Beijing (MA Photography and
               Digital Media)
Lives in Beijing
http://blog.sina.com.cn/u/1247299455

Solo Exhibitions

2005   Perfect Life: Photography by Liu Ren, Must Be Contemporary Art Center,
        Dashanzi Art District, Beijing, China

Selected Group Exhibitions

2006   Seoul International Photography Festival: Ultra Sense, South Korea
2006   Pingyao International Photography Festival, China
2006   Changing China, London Gallery West, University of Westminster, London, UK
2006   Object France, Centre Culturel Français de Pekin, Beijing, China
2006   Post Electronic Image, Must Be Contemporary Art Center, Dashanzi Art District,
        Beijing, China
2006   China/Chai-na, 706 Space, Dashanzi Art District, Beijing, China
2006   Festival Europeen de la Photo de Nu, Arles, France
2005   The Second Reality: Photographs from China, Berlaymont building,
        European Commission, Brussels, Belgium
2005   Life of New Beijing, New China, Central Academy of Fine Arts,
        Beijing (touring exhibition)
2005   Beijing Art Documenta – Jiang Hu, 799 Art Center, Dashanzi Art District, Beijing, China
2005   New Image China, Virginia Commonwealth University, Richmond, USA
2005   Only Child – Personal Record, Park 19 Art Space, Guangzhou, China

▲ Someday - Somewhere 04, 2005
◄◄ Someday - Somewhere 09, 2005

▲ Body, 2004
▼ Breakfast 06, 2004

LIU YI QING (YIKI) 刘 一青

- -

1982   Born in Shanghai

2000-2004   Shanghai University (Visual Communication)

Lives in Shanghai

www.liuyiqing.com

- -

Solo Exhibitions

2006   Shanghai Story, Freddie Fong Gallery, San Francisco, USA

2005   Flowness, Lianzhou International Photography Festival, China

2005   Green Exhibition: Face, Ag-Art Loft, Hangzhou, China / Tank
        Loft Arts Center, Chongqing, China

Selected Group Exhibitions

2006   Restless: Photography and New Media, Museum of
        Contemporary Art, Shanghai, China

2005   Sixth International San Francisco Photographic Art Exposition, USA

2005   Greation, Olive Hyde Gallery, San Francisco, USA

2005   Green Exhibition: Xfoto-Junk, Ag-Art Loft, Hangzhou, China / Tank
        Loft Arts Center, Chongqing, China

2005   Harvest: First Photography Exposition, Art Scene Warehouse, Shanghai, China

2005   Intimacy (Human People), Completely Naked at Campbell Works, London, UK

2005   Shanghai Camp Queen, First Lianzhou International Photography Festival, China

2005   Five New Generation Photographers, Epson Imaging Gallery -
        EpSITE Shanghai, China

2005   Selfhood-Absent Minded – Joint Exhibition of
        New Generation Photographers in China, Yiyun Town Arts Salon, China

17, 2002

▲ Q on the Sofa, 2001
▼ M & Z, 2002

LU YAN PENG　卢 彦鹏

1984　Born in Zhangzhou, Fujian Province
2001-2005　Art Academy of Fujian Educational College
Lives in Beijing

Selected Group Exhibitions

2005　Four Photographers, Exhibition Hall, Fujian Arts &
　　　Design College, Fuzhou, China
2003　Two Photographers, Fujian Arts & Design College, Fuzhou,
　　　China

Beijing Untitled series, 2006

Beijing Untitled series, 2006

PENG & CHEN 彭 和 陈

PENG YANG JUN 彭 扬军

1977   Born in Changsha, Hunan Province

1996-2000   Tianjing Industrial University (Fashion Design)

2006   Fabrica, Treviso, Italy

2005   Co-founder, Peng & Chen Studio

2001-2004   Creative director & chief photographer, Vision Magazine and Books

2000   Art director, Yifei Group

Lives in Shanghai and Beijing

www.peng-chen.com

CHEN JIAO JIAO 陈 皎皎

1980   Born in Beijing

1999-2003   Tsinghua University, Beijing (Communication)

2006-present   Fabrica, Treviso, Italy

2005   Co-founder, Peng & Chen Studio

2004   Editorial director, Vision City Books, Yifei Media

2003   Editor, Vision Magazine

Lives in Shanghai and Beijing

www.peng-chen.com

Solo Exhibitions

2004   Peng & Chen, Advance Art Center, Shanghai, China

Selected Group Exhibitions

2006   China Contemporary, Art, Architecture and Visual Culture,
Museum Boijmans van Beuningen, Rotterdam, the Netherlands

2006   Restless: Photography and New Media, Museum of
Contemporary Art, Shanghai, China

2006   Victime de la Mode - Fashion Victim, Crac Alsace, Altkirch, France

2005   Shanghai Cool, Shanghai Duolun Modern of Modern Art, Shanghai, China

2005   Get It Louder (touring exhibition)

2005   Biennale Montpellier-Chine, Montpellier, France

2004   Shanghai on Sale, Advance Art Center, Shanghai, China

▲ Flashlight series, undated
◄◄ Bed, 2004
◄◄◄ Suit, 2005

SHEN HAO 沈 浩

1980   Born in Shanghai

1998-2002   China Institute of Fine Art, Shanghai

2002   Co-founder, 0 Design Art Studio, Shanghai

2003-2004   L'Ecole Superieure Estienne (Typography), Paris, France

2004-2005   Universitie Paris 8 (Photography), Paris, France

2005-present   Project Photographer, Xintiandi-Shanghai

Lives in Shanghai and Paris

Projects

2006   Calligraphy in the Wind (installation with Yves Charnay),
         Shanghai Art Museum, Shanghai, China

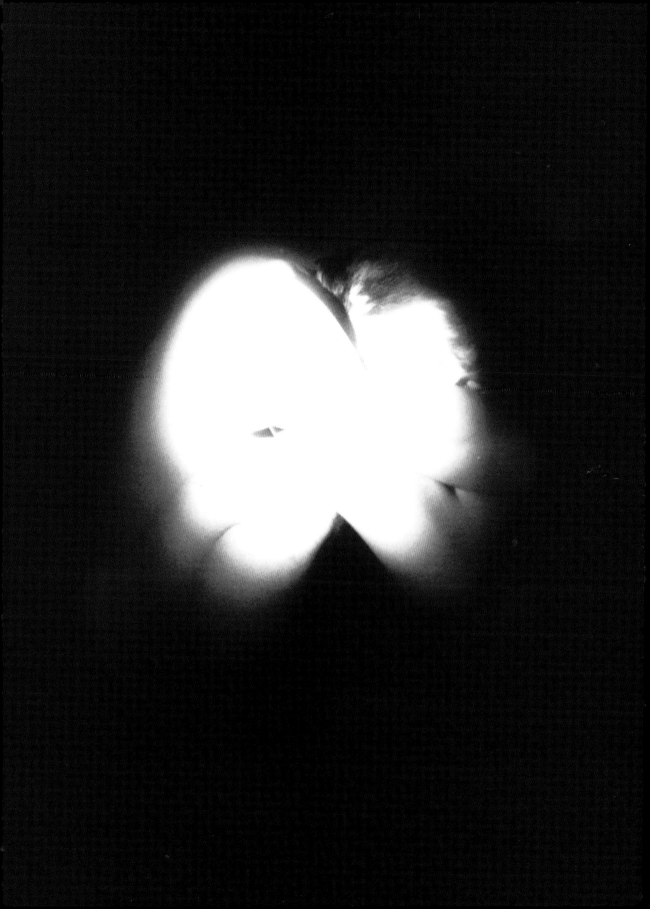

▶ Portrait, 2005
◀◀ Untitled, 2005

SI WEI (ZAO) 司 玮（早）

.

1980   Born in Hebei Province

2004   Co-founder, Perk Art and Design Studio

Lives in Shanghai

www.perk.cn

Selected Group Exhibitions

2006   Lu Xiang Annual Exhibition, Beijing, China

2005   Get It Louder (touring exhibition)

2005   Nike Free - New Media Exhibition, Shanghai, China

2005   SDF Taxi, temporary venue, Singapore

Pose (undated)

Solitude (undated)

Chinese Drama (undated)

SU HAN GUANG (ALEX)
苏 焊光

1978   Born in Guangzhou, Guangdong Province

2003-present   Creative Director, Modern Mobile Digital Media Group

2003-present   Founder and editor, ColdTea e-zine (www.ctmag.cn)

Lives in Guangzhou

Selected Group Exhibitions

2005   Selfhood-Absent Minded: Joint Exhibition of New Generation
Photographers in China, Lianzhou International Photography Festival,
China

Same Glasses Different Life, undated

◄◄ The New Generation Five, undated

At Home Alone

Water Float

TANG YI 汤艺

1982   Born in Chongqing, Sichuan Province

2000-2004   Sichuan Fine Art Institute (Oil Painting)

Lives in Beijing

www.tang-yi.cn

Solo Exhibitions

2005   Lemon Drop, Long March Space, Beijing, China

Selected Group Exhibitions

2006   Conversation 10+10, Shanghai Zendai Museum of Modern Art, China

2005   Body and Objects: Works by Chu Yun, Jiang Zhi, Tang Yi, Chambers Fine Art,
        New York, USA

2005   Archaeology of the Future: Second Triennial of Chinese Art,
        Nanjing Museum, China

2004   Strategy for Two Cities, temporary venue, Chongqing & Hong Kong SAR, China

2004   Unbounded, temporary venue, Chongqing, China

2004   Backpacker, temporary venue, Hong Kong SAR, China

2003   Enlarge, Alab Art Space, Kunming, China

2003   Eelectrolyte, Nanjing Shenghua Art Center, China

A Souvenir for Adolescence, 2006

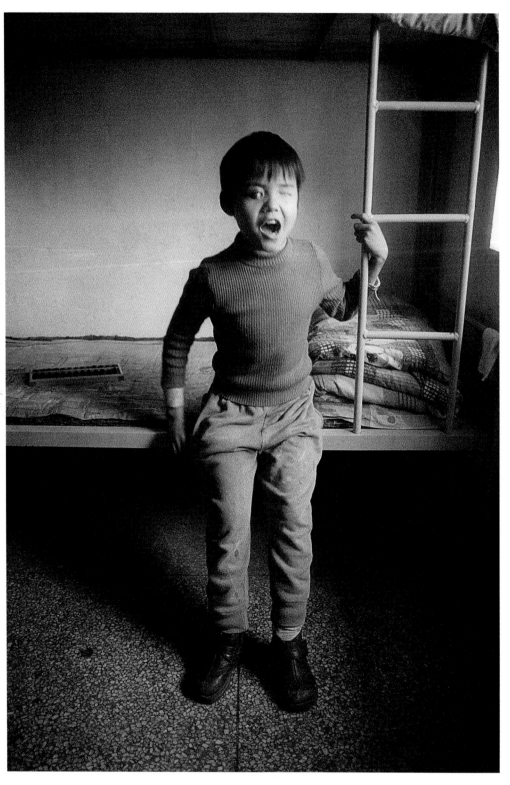

How Can You Hear Me? #26, 2003

How Can You Hear Me? #13, 2003

How Can You Hear Me? #9, 2003

How Can You Hear Me? #10, 2003

WANG YI FEI 王 一飞

1984   Born in Taiyuan, Shanxi Province
2004-present   Beijing Institute of Clothing Technology (Graphic Design)
Lives in Beijing

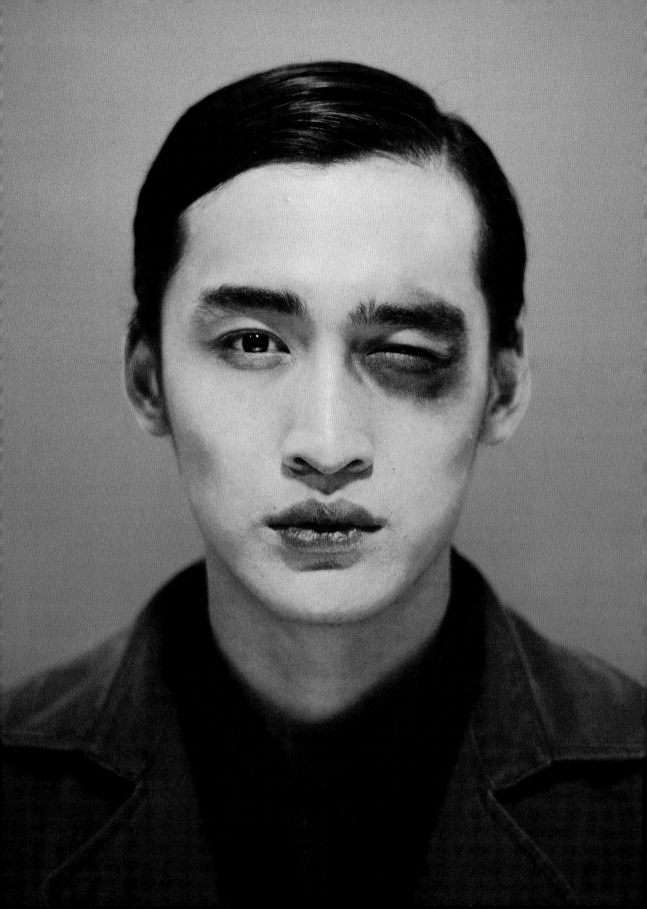

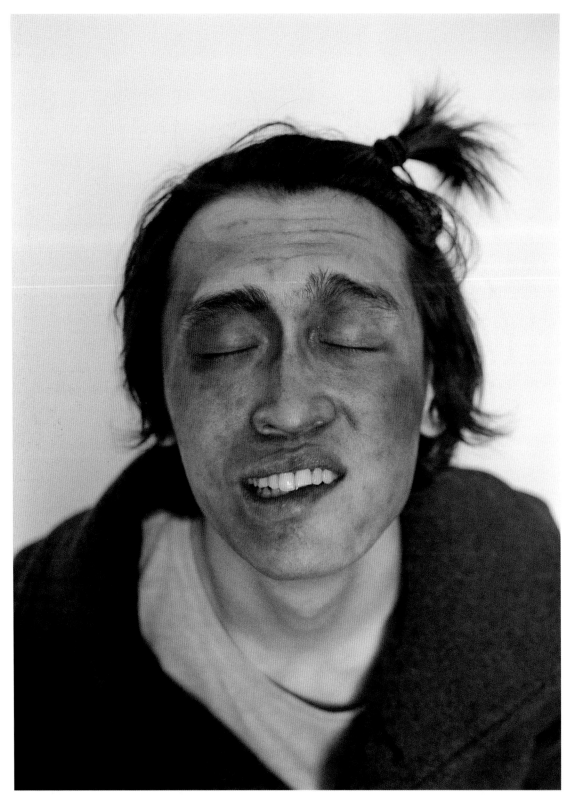

▲ Untitled Portrait, 2006
◄◄ Untitled Portrait, 2006

▲ Untitled Portrait, 2006
▼ Untitled Portrait, 2006

WEN LING (ZIBOY) 温 凌

1976   Born in Beijing

1996-2000   Central Academy of Fine Arts, Beijing (Printmaking)

2002-2003   Photographer, Beijing Times

2005   Co-founder, www.photoblogchina.com

Lives in Beijing

www.ziboy.com

Solo Exhibitions

2006   Here - Photoblogger Ziboy's Self Expression, Dimensions Art Center,
Beijing, China

Selected Group Exhibitions

2006   Luxiao Annual Exhibition, Star Gallery, Beijing, China

2006   Asia Contemporary Art Exhibition, Gwangju Biennale, South Korea

2005   Naughty Kids, 3818 Warehouse, Beijing, China

2005   Les Nuits Magiques – Festival International du Film d'Animation,
Bègles, France

2005   N12, Central Academy of Fine Arts, No. 3 Gallery, Beijing, China

2005   Street Tease, Bugis Street, Singapore

2005   Fourth Anniversary Starving Artists, Yan Club Art Center, Beijing, China

2005   A Cartoon? Taikang Top Space, Beijing, China

2005   Next Station: Cartoon? Star Gallery, Beijing

2004   N12, Central Academy of Fine Arts, No. 2 Gallery, Beijing, China

2004   One to One: Recent Photography from China, Chambers Fine Art,
New York, USA

2000   We, Contemporary Art Gallery, Beijing, China

2003.10.19

▲ 2005.10.1
▼ 2005.4.9

▲ 2005.7.24
▼ 2005.2.6

XU CHENG 徐 程

1980   Born in Shanghai

2000-2003   Donghua University, Shanghai (Media Art & Design)

2004   Founder, Xiang e-zine (www.gnaix.org)

Selected Group Exhibitions

2006   Restless: Museum of Contemporary Art, Shanghai, China

2005   Selfhood-Absent Minded: Joint Exhibition of New Generation

　　　　Photographers in China, Lianzhou International Photography Festival, China

2005   Mono, Shanghai Duolun Museum of Modern Art, China

2005   Nice Photos in a Museum, Mingyun Art Center, Shanghai, China

2005   Shandow Maker, Advanced Art Center, Shanghai, China

2004   Landscape, Loft 49, Hangzhou, China

Projects

2004   Curator, XCOPY001 Photo Exhibition, temporary venue, Shanghai, China

Library – Senscape series, 2005

Riverbed – Senscape series, 2005

Skeleton – Senscape series, 2005

Untitled, Streetscene series, 2004-2006

Untitled, Streetscene series, 2004-2006

XU ZI YU 徐 梓峪

1979　Born in Shanghai
1999-2003　Shanghai University of Fine Art
Freelance photographer
http://andrei.blogbus.com/index.html

Stalker series, 2002-2006

Stalker series, 2002-2006

YANG CHANG HONG　杨 长虹

1979　Born in Anshun, Guizhou Province

2000-2004　Photographer, Southern Metropolitan News

2004-2005　Photographer, Shenzhen Daily

2005-present　Photographer, Southern Metropolitan News

Lives in Guangzhou

Selected Group Exhibitions

2005　Ninth Guilin International Photography Festival, China

2005　Selfhood-Absent Minded: Joint Exhibition of New Generation
Photographers in China, Lianzhou International Photography
Festival, China

2004　10th Pingyao International Photography Festival, China

Leaving series, undated

Leaving series, undated
◄◄ Leaving series, undated

YAO YI CHUN   姚 轶淳

1984   Born in Shanghai
2002-2006   Chinese Academy of Art, Shanghai
Lives in Shanghai
http://naked.blogcn.com, www.dezen.net

Selected Group Exhibitions

2006   1800-0600, Epson Imaging Gallery – EpSITE Shanghai, China
2006   Outlook Art and Design, Supergrand Mall, Shanghai, China
2005   Streetsnaps, Room with a View Gallery, Shanghai, China

FUJI 100

Impression series, 2006

ZHANG JUN GANG (K1973) 张 君刚

1976   Born in Harbin, Heilongjiang Province

1999-2001   Heilongjiang University

2004-2006   Freelance photographer

Lives in Shanghai

www.k1973.com, http://sbhyh.blogbus.com

Selected Group Exhibitions

2006   Sixth Annual San Francisco Photographic Art Exposition, San Francisco, USA

2005   China Qingse, Ag-Art Loft, Hangzhou, China

2005   Private Image, Pingyao International Photography Festival, Pingyao, China

2005   Nice Photos in a Museum, Origin Cube, Shanghai, China

2004   Landscape, Loft 49, Hangzhou, China

▲ Song Hua River #1, 2006
▶▶ Shanghai Pudong #2, 2006

▲ Zha Long, 2006
▼ Shanghai Pudong #1, 2006

Zhu Jia Jian Island, 2006

ZHAO YAO 赵 要

- -

1981   Born in Luzhou, Sichuan Province
2000-2004   Sichuan Fine Arts Institute (Design Arts)
Lives in Beijing
www.blogcn.com/User12/zhaoxao/index.html

- -

Solo Exhibitions

2006   MOCA Envisage / Entry Gate: Chinese Aesthetics of Heterogeneity,
        Museum of Contemporary Art, Shanghai, China
2006   Six Photos and a Small Room, Long March Space, Beijing, China
2005   Rumor Décor, DDM Warehouse, Shanghai, China
2005   Spectacle: Century and Paradise, Second Chengdu Biennial, Chengdu, China
2005   Second Triennial of Chinese Art: Archaeology of the Future,
        Nanjing Museum, China
2004   Strategy For Two Cities, temporary venue, Chongqing & Hong Kong SAR, China
2003   Suspense, temporary venue, Chongqing, China

Young China, 2004

Day and Month in 2006 #1

Zhao Yao

Day and Month in 2006 #2

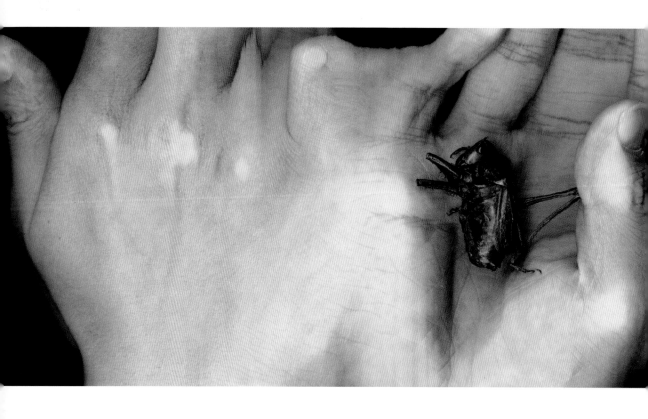

Right Hand 1, 2006

Right Hand 2, 2006

ZHENG ZHI YUAN 郑 知渊

1977   Born in Shanghai
2000-2003   Shanghai University of Engineering Science
Lives in Shanghai
http://san.blogbus.com

Selected Group Exhibitions

2006   Restless: Photography and New Media, Museum of
        Contemporary Art, Shanghai, China
2005   Three Years, Wangde Gallery, Shanghai, China

◄◄ Undercurrent series, 2006

Undercurrent series, 2006

The editor would like to thank all the photographers involved in this project for their brilliant cooperation and for their willingness to make this publication a significant showcase of new photography in China. Other artists who made an important contribution include Bai Chuan, Cai Hong Suo, Dai Mou Yu, Zong Ning, Zhou Hong Bin and Zhen Tao. Thank you all so much.

Grateful thanks are also due to all the professionals and friends that contributed to make this publication better, including Wenny Teo of the Museum of Contemporary Art, Shanghai, Shi Hantao of the EpSITE Gallery Shanghai, Carol Lu and Phoebe Wong of the Asia Art Archive, Brian Wallace of Redgate Gallery, Lorenz Helbling of Shanghart Gallery, Zhang Zhao Hui, Prof. John Clark, Phil Tinari, Lizzie Turner and Oscar Ho. This book would not have been possible without the generous advice of Johnny Cheng and the heroic efforts of all members of UNITAG Design: Yako, Men, Huan and Ken. Finally, a special thank you goes to all those whose influence and encouragement has been so important to this project, including Angelica Cheung, Hilary Binks, Ian Findlay-Brown, Jin Lam, Richard (for the electric toothbrushes), and Ann and Malcolm Millichap whose support is unwavering.

Pages 4-5: Birdhead World 2004-2005
Pages 6-7: Cao Fei, Diversionist, 2006
Pages 8-9: Liang Yue, Night Traffic, undated
Pages 12: Lin Zhi Peng (223), Bed, 2006

Published by 3030 Press, Unit 206A, Block B, Sea View Estates, 2-8 Watson Road
North Point, Hong Kong SAR
www.3030press.com
© 3030 Press

Designed by UNITAG www.unitag.cn

ISBN 988-99384-0-5
Printed in China